Premonition

poems by

J. M. Paden

Finishing Line Press
Georgetown, Kentucky

Premonition

Copyright © 2023 by J. M. Paden
ISBN 979-8-88838-380-3 First Edition
All rights reserved under International and Pan-American Copyright Conventions. No part of this book may be reproduced in any manner whatsoever without written permission from the publisher, except in the case of brief quotations embodied in critical articles and reviews.

Publisher: Leah Huete de Maines
Editor: Christen Kincaid
Cover Art: Nicole McGuire
Author Photo: Htet Cho Oo
Cover Design: Nicole McGuire and Elizabeth Maines McCleavy

Order online: www.finishinglinepress.com
also available on amazon.com

Author inquiries and mail orders:
Finishing Line Press
P. O. Box 1626
Georgetown, Kentucky 40324
U. S. A.

Table of Contents

Part One: Girl Visions

Perspective 1
Wild Child 2
Girlhood 3
Vampire Bites 4
Afternoon in November 5
Present & Past 7
How to know if your dad has cancer 9
June 27th 11
Don't lie down with the pigeons 12
If Your Right Hand Offends You, Deconstruct Your Religion 13
Grocery Store Love Poem 15
Twins 16

Part Two: Memory of the Future

Monopoly Junior 21
Where do we go from here 22
End of summer at your house 23
When the sun slips 24
With or Without You 25
Premonition 26
the day of the accident 27
I still have dreams about it 28
2am 29
First day of Spring 30
The Turtle Tells the Tortoise to Swim 31
The Ghosts of Fayette County Smoke Pall Malls on
    Sunday Morning 32
Blackberry Winter 33
No one ever told me, always 34
The Remains of the Poet Confront the Storm 35
Do-over 36

Part Three: Funeral March

A girl on fire 39
When we go for our walk, we see roadkill 40
I laughed at my abuser's funeral 41
The Kickback 42
Fighting His Ghost 43
Sunflower Trailer Park—Fairview, Mississippi 44
The Ice Castle 45
Snowden Grove Amphitheater (What Love Looks Like) 46
We 47
Cop Cars at Lamar and Central 48
Blue light thoughts before sleep 49
Wind & rain 50
It's all for you 51
Opryland after Aaron West 53
A day in September in a one-bedroom apartment 54
Lose the time 55
When Charlie dies two days before Christmas, we sit in the mud 56
Oak Box 57

Part Four: Rain

Worn out shoes 61
Anxiety in a High-Rise 62
On leaving my job 63
High-rise with rain 64

Acknowledgments 65

Author Bio 67

Part One: Girl Visions

Perspective

When the moon slipped
behind the trees
you told me it was magic.
Hold your hand up to the sky and catch it.
Take it in your palm and turn it
over and over and over—like a stone.
Hold the shadowed side
with bright eyes of knowing.
Rotation works its own kind of magic.
Flip it over in your hands and whisper
      a spell,
            a rule,
                  you told me
the moon does not hide
behind the branches.
We only blame it for our perception.
We blame it for its magic.
The way it makes us fumble
over our own human feet.

Wild Child

Bethany's mother forbade our playing in the field,
two little girls, wrinkled skinny-knees caked with mud.

Hunting season. Still, we tiptoed in the bean fields
looked for copperhead smiles between punchy rows of green.

The world felt huge,   a time far, far away
the farmland rolled out in front of us,   a wild child's invitation.

In the afternoon, we watched Peter Pan in Bethany's living room.
We flew to and fro in our imaginations.

It seemed so impossibly great
that God had let Peter be free.

Girlhood

the earth in its turning
meets me before I am ready

age 9, church parking lot
concrete scrapes skin

like licking icing off a cake
like I owe it a taste

ask daddy for band-aids
hidden somewhere in the sanctuary

he comes back empty handed

Vampire Bites

under the hickory tree in the backyard
the neighbor boy ate a spoonful of dirt
and told me it was proof
he was a vampire.
we played with the poison berries
fallen
from the tree and made pretend desserts.
never thought about how deadly they were.
my biggest fear was vampires—
too many Scooby-doo episodes
left me tucking my blankets all the way up
to protect my neck
while I slept.
I was sure some cloaked figure with fangs
would meet me through the closet door
in the dull light of a summer moon.

the neighbor boy disappeared one summer.
only returning once, a year later
to wave at my brother and I from the back
of his mom's green van.
another friendship lost to a sudden leaving,
and it was nothing like it used to be.

Afternoon in November

I can't hear anyone's talk.
The refrigerator is buzzing and
I have homework.
We're babysitting the neighbor's dog.

Daddy comes home around six thirty,
                                          or seven,
                                          or eight.
It's dark and raining hard
ting, ting on the metal roof.

Momma tells me I'm a lighthouse
but I'm not so sure.

Daddy talks about Big Brother
unlacing his work boots.
                              There's always someone to beat you
                              down, don't be the one to hand
                              over the bat.

Little sister's boyfriend moved
to Ohio for a job. She cuts
hair all day for women
who won't tell her
what they want.
Complains about her feet throbbing.
Takes the dog out for a walk.

Momma lost her keys, forgets.
Asks me three times if I checked
between the bedsheets.
The change in Daddy's pocket
jingles through the bedroom door.

Momma's in the kitchen.
I hear her every other word:
                              Obama, refugees

She trips over the neighbor-dog.
Daddy's voice is the cat's yawn,
                                    I know, I know.

I lay down in my tiny room.
Hear the tv that no one's watching
on the other side of the wall.

Voices hum in my ears.
It's raining harder now.

The carpet smells like urine
(from the neighbor-dog).
The refrigerator churns out a clump of ice

I count *ting, tings* on the roof
until I can't hold my eyes open.

Present & Past

I.
1.5 hours of sleep
in the bed with the wooden slats
hanging
loosely from the frame.
A child's bed but not my own.
My just-for-now
between
Memphis, Clarksville, home—and a life I am making
for myself on the banks of another muddy river.

II.
I've said it before: I came out swingin'
from the Tennessee backwoods.
My hair coated in red
clay mud—praying for a mind as flat as the delta.

III.
Chigger bites and honeysuckle-syrup-tongue.
Church pews and haunted houses in the woods.

IV.
We played restaurant under the holly tree
red poison berries for dessert, and
a chapter of Genesis behind
the back window. We ate
cornbread and mashed potatoes.
Listened softly, Momma's ghost stories
                    floating overhead.

V.
Insomnia: the incessant singing of the television.
Arm cradling head, begging for sleep.
Splashes of light circle behind
closed eyelids; I am five prayers
                    deep.
Voices sticking to the dark

corners like cobwebs. My nights always
a dance with memory. My mind

                                        a spiral, a penance, maybe.

How to know if your dad has cancer

you overhear him complain to your mom
you overhear him creak and groan in the middle of the night
he tells you about the aching that never   goes away
you try to think of ways   to make it better
you buy ice packs and supplements
new shoes to help his back
chocolate to help him numb, then
he tells you about the pain and you let him

he goes to the same doctor
he goes to a new one
he's referred to a specialist
he waits to catch their words and
he's told it would all go away if he just lost   a few pounds
                                                                               he sinks

he's told it's the knee replacement he had five years ago
he's told the plastic hinge slipped out of place
the specialist sends him for a biopsy
you go with him and work from the waiting room
the words swim—you try to keep your head above water and
you go home exhausted

two weeks later, they call and say leukemia
        they say chronic
        they say blood cells
        they say lymph nodes
        they say he'll manage
they say every little thing the cancer has a claim on, no matter what you do
you say: "I'm sorry"

you numb because you don't know how to keep going if you feel too much
you tell him you love him
you watch him bump and scrape around
you can see from the squint in his eye that he's afraid   of dying
                                                                                 of this being all there is

you keep cleaning the house
you keep working
you keep

you don't tell your boss because you want to stay professional, because
you can't stop talking about it once you start, so

you try not to start and

three months go by and

you have your first panic attack
there you are on the porch and

you suck in air like a vortex but you can't
                              breathe
you can't stop
                        wailing
you are heaving in every broken piece of yourself
cutting open from within

your dad finds you
he says he won't ask any questions
       but he's here
       but he's here
       his hand in yours and

you tell him it was a bad dream
you tell him white hot rage
you tell him you woke up feeling like a branding iron but

you don't know why

he sits with you the rest of Sunday morning
you never tell him it wasn't just a bad dream

June 27th

I shuffle and ask the cards if I'll

get into grad school

pipe dreams and the osculating fan

it's a joke to think

about but there is just a

sliver of moon left

                      in the sky

I think it might just

be enough

Don't lie down with the pigeons

Little girls,
if the pigeons
talk too much,
split them
with a string

don't be afraid
to break things

aren't we all
bursting open
anyway?

don't lie down
with the pigeons

this city
is swimmin'
in the birds of scrutiny

just because
your skin
is the glass
they see
you through

does not mean
you are only
skin

just because
nobody's listenin'
doesn't mean
you can't scream

if the pigeons
talk too much,

don't you dare
cut yourself open

Little girls,
tremble
if you must
but stand yourself up

back
to the bricks

and don't you ever
lie down

If Your Right Hand Offends You, Deconstruct Your Religion

I pray with one palm open / pick at the skin / peel back flesh / open and pink / wonder, rotate my knuckles / does the flesh consume me? / I coax out the blood / with a snake charmer's song / do I consume my flesh? / pull my muscles out one by one / like fat leeches / crack the bones / trace my tongue around the splinters / yank the shards out with my teeth

Grocery Store Love Poem

A young man and a young woman trade glances
under the buzz of produce section lights.
Speak over lifted arms, return fruit to the shelves.

Somewhere between the aisles a child is screaming
(there is always a child screaming)—
a protest to his mother.

The young man says, "You're beautiful."
The young woman laughs to the ceiling.
Places another bag of apples
on the slanted pile. "So are you."

> A man walks by with his toes pointing outward,
> demands bananas.

The young man tells him
it is the wrong time of day to expect bananas.

It is late enough that the crowds and the sun have rushed home
full of irritable reflections of the last few hours,
but not late enough for the truck to be in with fresh bananas.

> With a shake of his head, the man scoffs,
> leaves,
> mutters a word
> or two about never returning.

The young man turns back to the young woman
tilts his head just slightly
before the corners of her mouth slide up
into quiet laughter.

Twins

You are my mirror girl
you wake up from
I can take your hand
backhand

we are side by side
sometimes we ask each other
I want to be the one
Forest-eaten boots
I want to be the one
then look back up
and what I say is

what a loss we are
trying to put on each
my shoulders don't fit
your legs aren't quite strong
Where are

where does a girl end
how can we be ghosts
our mother

I write stories
and hope no one notices
I write stories
and hope I am not
but if I'm not
who does that leave

we are the same
at paper dolls
of girlhood
of the white oaks
how they soar
a sapling before
even thought of

the kind of good dream
steal the feeling to take with you
close it over mine
cuddled to your palm

which one are you?
the same
with the braided hair
you tell me
that our friends like more, I think
take your other hand
I want us to never be alone

to one another
other's skin
above your rib cage
enough to hold me up
you?

and a sister begin?
in these bodies
gave us?

about you
I am the main character
about ghosts
the main character
the main character
to haunt the pages?

and I am no good
these cliché things
I like the power
behind our house
up above me
our grandparents were
I love the flimsiness

of the bark
how you peal it back
but it loves

the whimsy in a tree's skin
to white bone
you, still

Part Two: Memory of the Future

Monopoly Junior

She likes to hold her Monopoly money.
She likes to count
the little dollar bills.

She likes to buy the boardwalk slots,
talk loudly—she won't bother
with anything less than five dollars.
The highest you can spend.

She squeals in a funny way
like her laugh has to crawl out of her nose.
Contorted, grinning face.
She giggles when someone has to pay
her rent.

Teacher sits back, wonders
if this will carry into her adultness
or if it's just
a third-grade peculiarity.

Precocious money handling
in fair, little hands.

Where do we go from here

the spot behind my eyelids is shot / in the dark, sad / like pouring the sun into bottles / throwing each out to sea / where do people go / to get their hope / where am I / when the sun reaches / its highest point in this sky / then decides it misses its lover and must return / to the cold side of the spinning rock / I have always stood alone / on one leg / in the middle of a small town / meteor shower / I am not afraid of vastness / ice and soot and the missing / sound bites in a static-lined phone—conversation / but where do we go from here / when we are friendly with only the air in our lungs

End of summer at your house

We're here listening to the frog songs.
75 degrees and dozing from the cough syrup.
Evening, too cool for the end of summer in the south.

Where do we go from here
but back to where we always go?

The comfortable, the comforted.
Maybe it's not so bad—or the end.

You can call mourning or jubilee.
It doesn't matter if you don't speak

the language. You're lost
in the pull of leaving light.

Maybe I'm just high from the rising
tent of sleep, warm breeze.

I tend to like endings
that hand over swaddled peace

and ask me to walk gently,
for—as clumsy as I am,

I do fall like feathers when I want to.

I want to go gently.

When the sun slips

we grope for firecrackers. Ashes
sweet. The grass blades confide in our ankles.

Whispers of the new July are here
and your body

                              an eternity
wrapped in dusty skin. The divide

between us holds today.
I breathe in smoke.

Crack my spine.
Remember me that way.

The sky rations the stars, and
all at once, we forget the persistence of the sun.

We focus on the missing:

the constellations I cannot fathom,
the tangles of heat and stardust.

My words are the lemonade
that tips out of hand.

Cold and bittersweet,
watering the worm's dirt.

Dust and bone and pollination.

Don't worry about next
July. It's always coming.

With or Without You

I remember the way February looks after midnight—
jigsaw lines of houses, small front yards
the rain crawling along the ground, turning to ice
speaking blacktop cracks into existence.

I remember your fingers reaching down my palm
until we meshed together
the heat of our skin, crossing of our fate lines
for better or worse.

an empty driveway
crabgrass stretching long limbs across the sidewalk
the hem of my shirt brushing the skin of my upper arm.

I remember lights burning above us
like spirits that couldn't part with our bodies
the persistence of the night
how my eyes begged me to close them
how I let them for a long moment when you kissed me goodnight
the echo, *text me that you made it home safe*
rolling the window down to feel the cold.

I remember the bass drum
how it still pulls on the walls of my gut
with or without you.

the rain and the cold air and the dark clouded sky
how we began to grow fuzzy
but still, more permanent as time barreled forward.

Premonition

On the day I almost die under the bumper of a Dodge RAM
my life does not flash before my eyes.

Instead, I hear the curling voices of my sisters.
Unintelligible. Words just a hum in my skull.

My body singing to itself—and only
to itself. A static song.

After my head splits open and my thoughts
pool out on the asphalt. My first words are
JesusJesusJesus
like a prayer but also like a siren
and everything else is silent.

I become keenly aware of purgatory.

The ambulance my confessional.
All my sins washing over my memory

until I can see nothing else
but the red blood of cleansing.
The punishment I gave myself.

When I told my friend something bad
was going to happen

in the days before the accident
I called it a premonition.

She said, *you worry too much.*

the day of the accident

(after "Flame" by C. D. Wright)

the breeze	the sunshine	the asphalt
the caution	the blind spot	the sweat
the fate	the squeal	the scrape
the clouds	the scream	the head
the concrete	the silence	the prayer
the flesh	the choke	the brakes
the fate	the left	the waiting
the lips	the voice	the black

I still have dreams about it

I wake up with sores
flesh open and raw from the air.
My throat closed up in my sleep,
my nostrils unable to pull
everything I need from the air.
A half dream whispering in my ear.
Panic swarming my skin,
sitting up in bed, dry eyes,
three hours of sleep

2am

I hear you brown—
eyelids collapse under streetlights.
No words
a brown pull
sidewalk chill, 2am.

You twist up my stomach
the way the earth bends the colors
of water
in crevices at our feet.

Cold skin…
you don't speak
but I listen,
bewitched.

I still remember
the warmth of your lips.

I hear you brown.
Your breath evaporates in the wind,
caressing visions,
as close as rain in the crooks of my body.

First day of Spring

A worm crawls under my skin
inching along, stretching.

Tennessee rains sunbeams
for the first time all year.

Even when the sun is out
my body makes clouds.

Sewage is gurgling
in the backyard.

We pretend we don't smell it
because the money isn't there.

I am a playground
for things that eat the dead.
I spoil everything.

Never thought I'd live
through the midnights of January.

But today, Tennessee is lighting up
green and yellow. The wind in the treetops.

The worms composting the dead, dead earth.

The Turtle Tells the Tortoise to Swim

I lose my footing
right as the rain begins
to pool

the daylight,
      the floods,
           all at once
my shell is sinking

      the turtle tells me: *that's how life works,*
      take another breath of freshwater
      his webbed feet ready

I'm flailing my limbs, trying to grow gills

my body is taking on water,
legs tied up in fisherman's knots

        him: full of ease   made for the water
    him: pulling oxygen   from under the surface
  him: a gully cut away   by good intentions

good enough for himself

whether I swing my limbs
until they fail me   or let the water overcome

my shell—

either way I'm filling my lungs—
to the brim—

ballooned, sunk

The Ghosts of Fayette County Smoke Pall Malls on Sunday Morning

Daddy craved smoke from twenty-nine
years ago in the soft light of February

dip in the road, the earth exhaled slowly
as we sloped down   between two hills

I had suspicions, small town testimonies
but never the words from his mouth

Daddy never told me   he ran around
but I kind of had the idea

he scowled under parking lot lights
when schoolmates said hi in passing

I never admitted when I liked a boy
though he must have seen it   a secret in my eyes

and still, my cheeks burn
when men speak to me   within his earshot
or not

a year after the smoke and hills and cool light
I crave wine
I am aching

for something to numb
without spoiling the vessel   without suspicion of anyone else

and in one more subtle, caressing way
I am just like my father

Blackberry Winter

May brings a chill in the air. It seems too normal
to comprehend. We feel as old as the dirt we plowed,

and a cold fog falls over our garden. Holes in the ozone close up,
bound to reopen. There are no cars on Summer Avenue.

Goodbyes whispered under a long-distance echo,
six feet and people in the streets. Thinking, and thinking,

and thinking: how will we explain this to our grandchildren?
Our great grandchildren? How the skies cleared over the city.

The wolves came out to roam the streets. And we howled.

How suddenly we could all breathe but were too afraid of catching.

No one ever told me, always

I always said: you have to split yourself
open down the middle where the juicy parts are
gotta let people worm their fingers between
gut and water and vein and leave yourself
like meat on a plate   just to leave
your mark, just to be like Jesus, I thought

Jesus, I thought you spoke louder than this, why?
why didn't you tell me I was a feeding ground
for creatures who smell of death, oh why
didn't I know to trust my own nose, is it
because I am only a shell
the vessel the spirit must do its work through
just the empty thing you had to fill with
nothing of my own

just oh so many clouds

why didn't you speak up before the flesh
was plucked clean from my bones
now dry, cracked rocks

The Remains of the Poet Confront the Storm

you leave my ocean
for your lover
only to return at break
of morning, glory brewing
unexpectedly churning my waters

grinding my skin, bones, lungs
into tiny bits, leftover

and when I finally wash
ashore in torn up parts

you're the one crying
you, always spilling over

if I were my whole self
I'd dry your tears with sand
I'd shove my ocean down your throat

Do-over

Winter was always her beginning.
The bare tree limbs, the bloodless bark

pale, felt like something of a cleansing.
She liked to sit on the park bench

in the sharp light and count backwards from a hundred:
ninety-nine, ninety-eight. It flattened her mind

when all the dowsing rods of her brain
were firing
$$\begin{array}{cc} \text{north} & \text{south} \\ \text{east} & \text{west} \end{array}$$

she supposed, winter, with its quiet streets
and chilled winds, which pushed all the noise

and all the colors indoors,
did something of the same.

Winter was a time when all living things
either slept or died, and all the people rushed away

and that   for her   meant a clean slate.
A do-over. A chance to mull it over—but

most of all: forget.

Part Three: Funeral March

A girl burning

Blaze me up like oil
and I'll reappear a spit fire light
in a rumpus, medias res
a lightning strike
flames in the grass
and once you cross me
all you'll see is heat waves
                flowing
in my wake

When we go for our walk, we see roadkill

the spine lays straight and flat against the concrete
with the intestines nestled at the base of the bones.

                    plump. full.

I laughed at my abuser's funeral

It seems like I'm not allowed
to call you   my abuser.

I can hear them saying
It was never   that bad

Did he rape you?   Did he force his way in or did I let him?
Did you give him the wrong idea?   Did I fall to the floor
                                      heaving in air
                                      hoping it was a dream?

What is the difference between rape and assault and why does anyone care?

Would you want his hands slipping into the valley
of your legs?
Would you hesitate and say "bottom" instead of butt
because "butt" implies you are too sexual?
Why should they believe you if your words seem sexual?
Would you wait two weeks before you told your parents?
Would you cry yourself to sleep when they still called him a friend?
And, so, the valley grows larger, your legs expand with guilt and the weight of self-hatred.
Are you fat *and* a whore now?
Do you hate yourself more?

But when a lady sits beside you on the pew
and says with a judgmental lilt in her voice

You seem happy.

You look down and feel ashamed all over again
You can't escape how free you feel
now that he's dead.

The Kickback

Me and Momma
hid in the big bathtub
      with his pistol
balanced on our kneecaps.

Clatter of my shaking   jaw
as loud as   the bullet crack.

Red of Momma's palm lines.
I read them easy.

Our fortune more clear
      with each of his footsteps.

 The breaking open
           bruised

skin of the world
split open.

        the blood
seeped thick
into his own
hands
    much deeper
    than any guilt

me and Momma
      felt in the kickback.

Fighting His Ghost

I'm having the nightmare:
he finds me in the back
of the funeral home and limps
towards me,
with that loose-limb-swing
like his legs are broken
some death-knell-dancing

but he has called up all his power
to catch me again.

you know you want this

Suggestion or command?
My chin like a dog's in his hand.

People are standing around the parlor
                the viewing area
standing over his corpse.

No one can see me
writhing out of his grip.

It's not the first time I've suffocated
in a full room

Sunflower Trailer Park—Fairview, Mississippi

Alice told me:
hippie lovers got old and anchored down,
here, under her sun,
and one white sky,
                                many moons ago.

They smoked cigarettes
like they would never run out,
asked her to clean the tops of window frames,
where they weren't nimble enough to reach.

If her mother was ever home,
she'd tell Alice not to clean the hippie mess.
Get a job. Help pay the rent.

I went there just to listen, Alice says.

We talk about leaving. About the hippies,
rabbit holes of poverty,
an apartment in New York City,
time   a train that never stops runnin'

and she says to me:
Eighteenth birthday is coming, Jenny.

in that ringin' tone of voice she uses,
when she talks about Fairview, Mississippi.

The Ice Castle

My hair freezes to the ground before they find me.

Momma chokes on the steam, pours warm water
into the frozen mud around me.

My brother stomachs the fullness of silence
waiting for the operator:
                         what is your emergency?

I am, I am, I am
a December chalk outline

dirty water swirling underneath the pull
of winter's moon

an empty space for good boys
who take my body

turn skin to frozen lake
like witchcraft, like backseat

fumbling me out
onto the hard dirt, into dawn

and in one night, I become

an ice castle
my brother finds built on the lawn.

Snowden Grove Amphitheater (What Love Looks Like)

Love likes to smoke cigarettes
in outdoor stadium seats.

When you're not the act it came for, it throws
words like axes, its curly grey hair,
broken and frayed—ends floating up in the breeze.

It shouts over your amplifier:
I don't know who you are
but I guess you're okay
and every head in the place
turns to Love and takes the cue—

You are unknown and unseen
by the one you've been trying
to catch for decades, since
fifth grade, the first boy you liked
with blond hair and kind eyes.
Since summers in church parking lots
and dark-skinned boys in the corner of your eye
waiting for the day they would finally
look your way
but they never did.

Love likes to be known, seen
to have you rub its back and run a bath for it.

But it doesn't always see you
with your knees dirt-kissed and stained
from setting up your own instruments,
ready to preform your set.

We

We speak in superlatives because we don't
know the rhythm of each other's
tongues. I love you more than anyone
has ever loved anyone, I don't care what you say.
Double tap, back bend
it feels like maybe we could close the distance
but this is a moment spinning in the sky—
no golden walkway, yet.
Could we be together?
No one has ever known
a love like ours, I'm telling you so.
You seem like me
you don't always seem
like someone I could get along with.
      The most. The best.
You seem like the one for me.
Where do I end
and we begin?

Cop Cars at Lamar and Central

The blue lights sprinkle the wall
from the window and all across the street.

We crash land on my bed.
It meets us in the air.

I pull the fluff of the comforter down
to see your stubbled cheek on the pillow.

We don't talk
but there's always that newborn smile in your eyes.
Sleepy, you let me cradle myself in the bend of your knees.

On the nights I don't have you
I hear a gunshot
and wonder if you're home yet.

The blue spin of the lights
come and go
I don't know—if I'm okay.

The pizza delivery guy waits at the gate.
Down the street someone delivers a splitting end
to a bullet.

There's a buzzing behind the south wall
of my bedroom, and I don't know if it's
the air conditioner or the city churning
                                          beneath me.

The streets lit up and burning
blue.

Blue light thoughts before sleep

When I say, *how are you*, I mean, please don't forget
who you are to me.

When I say, *I love you,* I'm hoping to hear you say
you never stopped loving me.
What a great couple we are—every whimper drowned out
by the next text message.

I forgot how to breathe, how exhaling tells the world
                                    who I am.

I forgot to release.
I can tell myself stories, lay myself down with faith
but tomorrow is a spaceship.

I wake up floating.

Where do people go to get their faith?

Wind & Rain

The wind jostles the windows of the car
                the rain
                  trickles down
into the arms of a puddle.
Tap, tap, tap, against the glass,

I think of you   hundreds of miles away.
What is the night like jutting up against your sky?

Flowers closing against the cool of the evening
the grass, garter snakes, screech owls watching
                              over you
    from the car, to the porch   up to the screen door.

Here, students come and go
in the apartment complex   across the street
the sky is foggy, gray-black, backlit by Memphis neon.

I cannot see the stars for the streetlights.

You're far away, but I like to think
of you humming, drumming the steering wheel
on the long drive across town.

Cradled under your sky.

It's all for you

I read aloud to you
as we sit in the Starbucks booth.

Empty tables—everywhere
sunlight pouring through.

This is how I say *I love you:*

I curl my tongue around each syllable.
The sway and swing of my lips.
My Tennessee chorus.

Summer and sunshine and lemonade.

I say it in the way I read the page.
Try to put poetry and color in the air
for you—it's all for you.

I paint each moment brighter
even as my raincloud drizzles on
the path behind—I say

I love you: bare and open.
I write it from the tips of my fingers.

On your neck
on lips pressed to skin.

I say it when I say *I miss you*
and pretend your hand's in mine.

I say it silent.
I say *I love you* as I fall again,

looking over at you
in our little Starbucks booth.

This: our world.
Everything else empty.

Opryland after Aaron West

I'm walking on stilts in the bookstore
chaos as a motion as a background drum
beat   only I can hear,
the intercom   I expect someone to tell me
I'm in the way, again, stop
and go conversations, half
acquaintances stand in the back
and shuffle peg-feet-swivel-neck
click-clack the stilts underfoot,   look up
don't look anyone in the face

I am a periphery person
if I get high enough
maybe I'll turn into a bat

maybe I'll vomit black
and my skin will stain

A day in September in a one-bedroom apartment

my finger falls between
socket and plug.
the jolt leaves me thinking
singed skin, numb fingers,
the blue blood drum of my heartbeat.

sit on the bed,
shiver when I blink.
think of heat,
a waving flame

burning a house in December
us barefoot, swaying with the light

a heart stopping
when there's no one
to call the ambulance.

I press my finger to my lips,
kiss the nail.

flashes of sunlight
on the street
barely reach me
through the open window.

Lose the time

on the weekends, I lay in bed and read *The New Yorker*.
I lay in bed and look at a screen
lay in bed and groan   and creak.
I whine as I straighten the heating pad.

I hung a cloth over the bed yesterday.
It rustles in the night against
the pale wall.
I think of women in red, how they peer over me
looking for something to eat.

My bones still hold the juicy sinews of childhood
yet every year I grow older, and I lose all the time.

When Charlie dies two days before Christmas, we sit in the mud

By the dog house, I press
hands to your heart, smooth your fur.

This is no mystery. A common moment.
Breathing, breathing, breath turning to fog

your heart stops and your eyes dot,
and all at once you are in a place that I have never been.

My nose drips, the grief comes
with clenched eyelids, jaw grinding.

The ground beneath me becomes the ocean floor, the pressure
lapping at my ears, pushing my skull in on itself.

I know what loss is.
The chasm of a heart cracked open.

The water floods in.
I relearn how to swim.

Oak Box

I brought your ashes home   in the oak box.
Lulling you in my lap, like you were a small thing
again, an inkling,   I hate thinking of you
closed up in the fawny wood
on the bookshelf.

The remnants of you   I pushed against my collar bone.

My family bickered on the way home, in the McDonald's drive-through
    common moments you know nothing of.

You are like a deer: light feet
your smile the slope of tall grass.

you are soft,   but restless
    hardly ever bedding down.

Loved.

    Are there fields in the after? Can you fill your lungs,
then let them collapse without a tremor?

Part Four: Rain

Worn out shoes

Slit in the sole.
The Achilles' heel.

Hidden rubber underbelly.

Losing.

Her heel peeking out.
The skin winking.
Her lifted body.

Anxiety in a High-Rise

the stairwell smells like a barbeque joint and also a joint; a lightbulb on the last flight of stairs is out and if the broken doorknob at the bottom of the darkness is any indication, the light will stay busted for months on end. So, I shove my shoulder into the heavy six coats of paint, rush through the door into the hallway, across from the mini-gym, mostly from the momentum but also from a general anxiety about meeting any fellow tenants in this space. I round the corner and weave between the two blueberry-cake colored couches in the lobby and stand in front of the vending machine—reach indecision, think about how chocolate hurts my teeth, and too much salt gives me a headache, listening to a Coke can hit the bottom of the machine as loud as the garbage trucks lifting dumpsters on Tuesdays at 4am. I buy the chips anyway, watch the bag fall. The stairwell door is too hard to open from this side without a doorknob, so I click the elevator button and even though the digital monitor tells me one elevator is available, I still wait eight minutes for the occupied elevator to empty on some unseeable floor. Wait, wait, wait. Listen to the box drop, then show up in front of me, not by choice, and I wish deeply and profoundly that maintenance would fix the doorknob. I like to leave my apartment without the risk of strangers occupying this steel box with me—also without people *I know* occupying the box with me—also—without having to wait this long—for the relief that should have fallen over my body already.

On leaving my job

I'll just call this a homecoming.
Maybe some of us are meant

for silence. For empty hallways, for
longing glances in the short moments

on the precipice of new mercies.
I'll finally come back to myself

after being quiet for so long, but—

there won't be anything to say
only to listen
two captivated ears.

High-rise with rain

we shadowed figures
run fully   awash
in parked car lights

lightning sharp   and bright
as if it were laughter
thunder like breath
sucked in
fills the purged caverns
inside us, all of us

together,   under
raindrops   held
by the window's cradle
we ring our hair   of the dark
speak   in shivers,
    wish for summer

losing   bits of sun

slipping moments

of a March   afternoon

Acknowledgments

A big thank you to the literary magazines and editors who held space for these poems. Earlier versions appeared in:

Barren Magazine—"Afternoon in November"; "Anxiety in a High-Rise"; "With or Without You"
The Shore Poetry—"Where do we go from here"
The Bookends Review—"End of summer at your house"
Every Pigeon—"A day in September in a one-bedroom apartment"
Ink & Nebula—"Don't lie down with the pigeons"
Ghost Bible—"2am"; "Opryland After Aaron West"
Okay Donkey—"First day of Spring"
Distance Yearning—"The Ghosts of Fayette County Smoke Pall Malls on Sunday Morning"
Tarot Literary—"The Remains of the Poet Confronts the Storm"
Versification—"When we go for our walk, we see roadkill"
Foothill: A Journal of Poetry—"The Kickback"
Pulp Poets Press—"The Ice Queen"
Ghost City Press—"Cop Cars at Lamar and Central"

A heartfelt thank you to Kendra Vanderlip and Lynne Schmidt for their friendship and feedback. Thank you to Jen Campbell and Niki Flowers for their stellar editing skills. Many thank you's to the professors who saw these poems in earlier versions and encouraged me as a writer—Dr Kathy Lou Schultz, Sonja Livingston, and Courtney Miller Santo.

Thank you to Momma, Daddy, Hannah, Buck, and Becca for the love. Thank you Logan Connor and Grammie for every smile you have put on my face. There would be no poems without both the light and the dark. Thank you.

J. M. Paden (she/her) is a writer, content marketer, and book reviewer from Memphis, TN. Her work has been published by *Foothill: A Journal of Poetry, Ghost City Press, Okay Donkey, Pulp Poets Press, The Bookends Review, The Financial Diet, Harbor Review*, and others. She is the founding editor of *Antipoetry Magazine* and writes a book review column called *Page Peeks*.

She grew up in backwoods Tennessee, then earned an BA in English from The University of Memphis in 2016. She believes the stories of poor southerners are complicated and deserve to be told. Much of her work reflects the grit, magic, and chaos fed to her straight from her southern roots. Her role models include The Cheshire Cat, Kim Possible, and Louise Belcher.

When she's not writing, she's trying to finish an endless stack of books or read her cats' impenetrable minds, each a worthy task as far as she's concerned.

Connect with her on X: @AntipoetryMag.

www.ingramcontent.com/pod-product-compliance
Lightning Source LLC
Chambersburg PA
CBHW020341170426
43200CB00006B/456